CRA

(CLINICAL RESEARCH ASSOCIATE)

HUMOR

IRENE XANDERENA

ISBN: 979-8-8689-3475-9

Published by
Eyereneeswords
Email: life@eyereneeswords.com
Website: www.eyereneeswords.com

CONTENT

CRA (CLINICAL RESEARCH ASSOCIATE) HUMOR

ACKNOWLEDGMENT

I would like to express my utmost gratitude to all the clinical research associates out there who inspired this book, for their unwavering dedication to science and their ability to find humor in even the most challenging of trials.

Your contributions to the medical field are truly remarkable, and I hope this book brings a smile to your face after a long day of data monitoring and protocol deviations. Your patience and ability to laugh at my questionable humor is a true testament to your resilience in the face of FDA regulations and source document discrepancies.

INTRODUCTION

I started writing the "Humor" series in 2023 because individuals tend to approach life and their careers with great seriousness. But once they grasp the concept that life is akin to a game, they will find it more pleasurable.

Now, I know what you're thinking; "Why in the name of double-blind studies would anyone write a humor book about data-crunching heroes?" So, let me enlighten you. I have taken it upon myself to write a humor book about the fascinating world of clinical research associates. I know what you're thinking, "Clinical research? Humor? Are you mad?" Well, perhaps a little mad, but hear me out. You see, behind those serious faces lies a treasure trove of hilarity that is begging to be unleashed.

These brilliant minds of science are the unsung comedians of the research world. Get ready to discover a side of clinical research that you never knew existed – the side that will leave you in stitches and wondering just how these researchers manage to keep a straight face in the face of such comedic chaos.

After spending countless hours in the world of clinical research, I realized that laughter truly is the best medicine. From deciphering incomprehensible medical jargon to surviving never-ending meetings, I couldn't help but document the hilarity yet excitement of being a clinical research associate.

A Clinical Research Associate (CRA) is a professional who oversees and monitors clinical trials conducted in medical research. They ensure that trials are conducted in compliance with regulations, protocols, and ethical guidelines while collecting and analyzing data to ensure the safety and efficacy of new treatments or interventions.

Have you ever wondered what happens behind the scenes of clinical research? Well, let me tell you, it's a comedy show waiting to happen! From chasing down elusive study participants like they are celebrities to battling the dreaded paperwork monster, being a clinical research associate is like being part detective, part spy, and part circus performer. So, in an attempt to preserve my sanity and share a few laughs, I couldn't resist writing a humor book about the wonderfully weird world of CRAs.

PREFACE

"What is research but a blind date with knowledge?"
@ *Professor Will Harvey*

In an effort to lighten the sometimes serious and complex world of clinical research, I decided to write a humor book specifically focused on the quirks and experiences of clinical research associates. By infusing humor into the anecdotes and situations faced by CRAs, I hope to provide a lighthearted perspective on their work while still acknowledging the importance and expertise required in this field.

This book aims to bring a smile to the faces of CRAs and anyone interested in the behind-the-scenes world of clinical research. In writing this humor book, I want to shed light on the often overlooked and underappreciated role they play in the field of healthcare.

With their meticulous attention to detail and endless paperwork, CRAs face unique challenges that deserve recognition in a light-hearted and entertaining way.

Through humorous anecdotes and relatable puns, I hope to bring laughter and appreciation to CRAs, and anyone interested in clinical research. Grab your lab coat and get ready as we delve into the wild and wacky world of CRAs. You will giggle your way through the trials and tribulations of the life of a clinical research associate one hilarious anecdote at a time! Let's Go!

CRA
(CLINICAL RESEARCH ASSOCIATE)
HUMOR

1

Why did the clinical research associate refuse to take the placebo?

Because they wanted to be the control group!

2

What did the clinical research associate say when they found out the trial drug was a placebo?

"Well, that's a bitter pill to swallow!"

3

Why did the clinical research associate go to the gym during a trial?

To work on their placebo effect!

4

How many clinical research associates does it take to change a light bulb?

None, they just document the change in the protocol and submit it to the sponsor for approval.

5

Why did the clinical research associate cross the road?

To get to the investigational site on the other side!

6

How do clinical research associates cook their meals?

They follow the protocol to the letter, of course!

7

Why did the clinical research associate become a CRA?

Because they wanted to monitor stuff!

8

How did the clinical research associate get over their fear of needles?

They enrolled in a clinical trial!

9

Why did the clinical research associate get into an argument with the study coordinator?

Because the study coordinator didn't follow the protocol!

10

Why did the clinical
research associate refuse to
take a bribe?

Because they knew it
would be a serious protocol
violation!

11

How do you know if a clinical research associate is having a bad day?

They start hallucinating about CRFs!

12

Why did the clinical research associate refuse to take a sick day?

Because they didn't want to risk a protocol deviation!

13

How many clinical research associates does it take to change a light bulb?

None! That's not in the protocol!

14

Why don't clinical research associates trust atoms?

Because they make up everything!

15

Why did the clinical research associate enroll in a clinical trial?

To experience what it's like to be a subject for once.

16

How many clinical research associates does it take to screw in a light bulb?

None! They're too busy monitoring!

17

How do clinical research associates like their coffee?

Blinded, randomized, and with a placebo shot of cream!

18

Why did the clinical research associate refuse to take a break?

Because they didn't want to risk missing any data!

19

What does a clinical research associate call a site that always meets their enrollment goals?

The miracle house!

20

Why did the clinical research associate get excited at the sight of a blank CRF?

Because they love a good challenge!

21

How do clinical research associates celebrate the end of a successful trial?

By going home and getting a good night's sleep!

22

What's the difference between a clinical research associate and a detective?

A clinical research associate doesn't need to solve a crime, just find the truth!

23

Why did the clinical research associate wear a lab coat to the site visit?

To look official and impress the study team!

24

How do clinical research associates keep their sanity during a challenging trial?

By reminding themselves that it's all for the greater good of scientific research!

25

Why did the clinical research associate bring a ladder to work?

Because they were always "climbing" up the hierarchy of clinical trials!

26

Why did the clinical research associate become a detective?

Because they were skilled at "investigating" data discrepancies and finding the truth!

27

Why did the clinical research associate always have a magnifying glass?

Because they had a keen eye for details and were experts at "examining" study protocols!

28

Why did the clinical research associate become a tightrope walker?

Because they were great at "balancing" the demands of multiple studies and deadlines!

29

How can you pick out a clinical research associate at a vacation retreat?

You will hear them reciting the entire protocol in their sleep but try asking them what they had for breakfast, they can't remember!

30

How can you tell if a clinical research associate is having a nightmare?

You hear them repeating visits backward! COV! RMV! SIV! SQV!

31

Why did the clinical research associate join a gym?

Because they needed to stay fit and "exercise" their critical thinking skills during data analysis!

32

Why did the clinical research associate have a garden?

Because they were always "cultivating" new studies and trials!

33

Why did the clinical research associate become a professional juggler?

Because they were skilled at "balancing" multiple projects and timelines.

34

Why did the clinical research associate always have a toolbox nearby?

Because they were masters at "fixing" any issues that arose during a study!

35

Why did the clinical research associate become a mathematician?

Because they were always "calculating" the perfect sample size for their studies!

36

Why did the clinical research associate become a motivational speaker?

Because they knew how to "inspire" their clinical research coordinators to achieve research goals with enthusiasm!

37

Why did the clinical research associate bring a microscope to the party?

Because they wanted to "study" the bacteria on the buffet!

38

Why did the clinical research associate go to the comedy club?

Because they needed a break from all the serious "data crunching" and wanted a good laugh!

39

Why did the clinical research associate become a magician?

Because they had the "magic touch" when it came to resolving data discrepancies!

40

Why did the clinical research associate become a chef?

Because they were great at "cooking up" innovative study designs and protocols!

41

Why did the clinical research associate become a detective?

Because they were always searching for the missing data!

42

Why did the clinical research associate join a band?

Because they wanted to conduct a "clinical trial" on the effects of music on patient well-being!

43

Why did the clinical research associate bring a ladder to work?

Because they were always "climbing" up the hierarchy of regulatory approvals!

44

Why did the clinical research associate go on a diet?

Because they needed to "weigh" the importance of data accuracy!

45

Why did the clinical research associate bring a stopwatch to the party?

Because they were always timing everything, even their social interactions!

46

Why did the clinical research associate always carry a magnifying glass?

Because they were experts at finding the tiniest discrepancies in data!

47

Why did the clinical research associate become a yoga instructor?

Because they needed to find a balance between the strict regulations and the flexibility required in clinical research!

48

Why did the clinical research associate become a circus performer?

Because they were experts at juggling multiple trials and deadlines!

49

Why did the clinical research associate start a gardening club?

Because they knew how to cultivate successful clinical trials just like they cultivated plants!

50

Why did the clinical research associate always have a map in their office?

Because they were skilled at navigating through complex regulatory pathways!

51

Why did the clinical research associate join a hiking group?

Because they were used to climbing mountains of paperwork and regulations!

52

Why did the clinical research associate join a dance class?

Because they were great at performing the data dance, ensuring accurate collection and analysis.

53

Why did the clinical research associate bring a notebook to a comedy show?

Because they were always ready to "note" down any potential side-splitting adverse events!

54

Why did the clinical research associate decide to experiment with comedy?

Because they wanted to see if humor could be a viable treatment option for study participants' stress levels!

55

What did the clinical research associate say to the study coordinator at the end of a long day?

"I could use a clinical trial of coffee to assess its efficacy in keeping me awake during data analysis!"

56

Why did the clinical research associate become a musician?

Because they wanted to conduct a symphony of data analysis!

57

What did the clinical research associate say to the coordinator about the study participant who kept forgetting to take their medication?

"Looks like we need to conduct a double-blind study on their memory!"

58

What do clinical research associates do when they can't find any adverse events?

They start a study on the mysterious disappearance of adverse events!

59

Why did the clinical
research associate
bring a parachute to the
investigator meeting?

Just in case the study results
were so mind-blowing
that they needed to make a
quick escape!

60

Why did the clinical research associate always carry a notepad and pen?

Because they didn't want to miss a "note-worthy" finding!

61

Why did the clinical research associate bring a stopwatch to the investigator meeting?

To make sure everyone adhered to the study timelines, of course!

62

How many clinical research associates does it take to change a lightbulb?

None, they simply start monitoring the effects of different lighting conditions on study participants!

63

Why did the clinical research associate become a detective?

Because they loved uncovering the truth behind data inconsistencies!

64

Why did the clinical research associate always carry a magnifying glass?

To "investigate" any suspicious data discrepancies!

65

Why did the clinical research associate bring an umbrella to the clinical site?

Because they always knew it would be a "site" for sore eyes!

66

Why did the clinical research associate have a collection of colorful pens?

To add some "colorful" creativity to their study documents!

67

Why did the clinical research associate always have a snack in their pocket?

Because they believed in the power of "trial and error" – especially when it came to finding the perfect snack!

68

Why did the clinical research associate start a band?

Because they knew how to "harmonize" different study teams and bring them together!

69

Why did the clinical research associate become a comedian?

Because they wanted to find out if laughter could be a clinical trial!

70

Why did the clinical research associate always carry a stopwatch?

Because they knew that time was of the "essence" when it came to meeting study deadlines!

71

Why did the clinical research associate bring a compass to work?

Because they never wanted to lose their "direction" in conducting trials!

72

Why did the clinical research associate bring a bag of ice to the clinical site?

Because they believed in the power of "cooling down" any heated debates during study meetings!

73

Why did the clinical research associate become a beekeeper?

Because they knew how to handle the "buzz" of multiple study sites!

74

Why did the clinical research associate always have a lab coat with them?

Because they believed in the saying, "Dress for success, even in the world of clinical trials!"

75

Why did the clinical research associate bring a microscope to their house party?

Because they wanted to make sure everyone was properly "observed" and documented!

76

Why did the clinical research associate always carry a notepad and pen?

Because they were constantly jotting down notes and documenting everything like a human recorder!

77

Why do clinical research associates make perfect meals from recipe books?

Because they know a recipe is just like a protocol you must follow the instructions perfectly.

78

Why did CRAs choose this profession?

To speak in acronyms using the RMV, IRB, GCP, AE, PD, IM, ROT, DOR, FDF, SIV, CCG, SQV, and COV that only CRAs understand.

79

How do clinical research associates stay calm under pressure?

They find the perfect placebo to keep their stress level in check.

80

What do you call a clinical research associate who loves to dance?

A trial-and-error dancer.

81

How do clinical research associates deal with difficult sites?

They use their placebo trial and error effect to charm site staff.

82

Why did the clinical research associate refuse to eat at a fast-food restaurant?

Because they were worried about the potential adverse events from the food.

83

How did the clinical research associate measure time?

They used subject enrollment as their unit of measurement.

84

Why did the clinical research associate bring a measuring tape to the site?

To measure the success of the trial in inches.

85

How does a clinical research
associate unwind over
the weekend?

They participate in
a placebo-controlled
Netflix marathon.

86

What excuse does a clinical research associate give when they don't want to go out?

Sorry, I can't go out. I have a strict screening and randomization schedule tonight.

87

Why did the clinical research associate bring a calculator to the beach?

To calculate the effectiveness of sunscreen application frequency based on SPF and body surface area.

88

How does a clinical research associate start their day?

By checking if their coffee is statistically significant in improving productivity for the day.

89

How does a clinical research associate stay organized?

They use a lot of trial
and error!

90

How do clinical research associates handle discrepancies?

They just keep digging until they find the truth.

91

How do clinical research associates handle protocol deviations?

They take a deep breath and remember that a deviation is just a temporary detour on the road to success!

92

Why did the clinical research associate become a detective?

To solve the mystery of unexpected study outcomes.

93

What is a clinical research associate's favorite way to relax?

Taking a placebo break and pretending they are in a control group.

10 REASONS WHY CLINICAL TRIALS ARE IMPORTANT

1. **Development of new treatments:** Clinical trials are essential for testing the safety and effectiveness of new medications, therapies, and medical procedures.

2. **Improved patient outcomes:** By participating in clinical trials, patients have access to potentially life-saving treatments that may not be available otherwise.

3. **Advancement in medical research:** Clinical trials contribute to expanding scientific knowledge, leading to discoveries that can positively impact future healthcare practices.

4. **Personalized medicine:** Through clinical trials, researchers can identify specific factors

that influence treatment effectiveness, leading to more tailored and individualized care.

5. **Safety evaluations:** Trials help identify potential side effects, risks, and complications associated with new medications or interventions, ensuring patient safety.

6. **Validation of existing treatments:** Trials not only assess new treatments but also evaluate the efficacy and safety of existing ones, providing more evidence-based information for healthcare decisions.

7. **Disease prevention and early detection:** Clinical trials play a vital role in identifying effective strategies for disease prevention, as well as developing better diagnostic techniques to detect conditions at earlier stages.

8. **Health disparities reduction:** By including diverse populations in clinical trials, healthcare

providers can address gaps in treatment access and effectiveness among different ethnicities, genders, and socioeconomic backgrounds.

9. **Collaboration and knowledge-sharing:** Clinical trials foster collaboration among researchers, healthcare providers, and patients, leading to the exchange of ideas and sharing of best practices.

10. **Innovation and progress:** Ultimately, clinical trials drive medical innovation, pushing the boundaries of what is possible in healthcare and leading to continuous advancements in medical science.

10 BENEFITS OF PARTICIPATING IN CLINICAL TRIALS

1. **Access to innovative treatments:** Clinical trials provide an opportunity to access cutting-edge treatments and therapies that may not be available through standard care options.

2. **Potential for improved medical outcomes:** By participating in clinical trials, patients may experience improved health outcomes, including better symptom management, disease control, or even potential disease remission.

3. **Close monitoring and care:** Participants in clinical trials receive close monitoring and care from a dedicated team of healthcare professionals throughout the study, ensuring comprehensive support and timely intervention.

4. **Contribution to medical knowledge:** By volunteering for a clinical trial, individuals contribute to the advancement of medical knowledge, helping researchers and scientists develop better treatment options for future patients.

5. **Access to expert medical advice:** Participants have the opportunity to work closely with experienced medical professionals who specialize in the specific condition or treatment being studied, providing valuable insights and guidance.

6. **Potential for early access to future treatments:** In some cases, clinical trial participants may gain early access to promising treatments that are not yet available to the general public.

7. **Financial support:** In certain clinical trials, participants may receive financial compensation

for their time and travel expenses, which can be a beneficial aspect for some individuals.

8. **Close monitoring of health status:** Regular check-ups and tests involved in clinical trials can help participants stay vigilant about their health, potentially leading to the early detection of other conditions or concerns.

9. **Emotional support and camaraderie:** Clinical trials often provide a support network of fellow participants, creating a sense of community and shared experiences, which can be comforting and empowering.

10. **Personal fulfillment:** Many participants find a sense of satisfaction and fulfillment by actively contributing to medical research and potentially making a difference in the lives of others facing similar health challenges.

10 REASONS TO TRUST YOUR CLINICAL RESEARCH ASSOCIATE (CRA)

1. **Expertise and knowledge:** CRAs are highly trained professionals with extensive knowledge of clinical research regulations, protocols, and procedures. They have the expertise to ensure that the study is conducted in compliance with ethical and regulatory standards.

2. **Attention to detail:** CRAs are meticulous in their work, paying close attention to every aspect of the study. They carefully review study documents, data, and records to ensure accuracy and reliability.

3. **Ethical conduct:** CRAs adhere to strict ethical guidelines in their work. They prioritize patient safety, informed consent, and confidentiality,

ensuring that participants' rights and well-being are protected throughout the study.

4. **Communication skills:** CRAs possess excellent communication skills, enabling them to effectively communicate with study participants, investigators, and other stakeholders. They can explain study procedures, address concerns, and provide updates in a clear and understandable manner.

5. **Organization and time management:** CRAs are skilled in managing multiple tasks and deadlines. They create and maintain detailed study plans, schedules, and documentation, ensuring that all activities are carried out in a timely and efficient manner.

6. **Problem-solving abilities:** CRAs are trained to identify and address any issues or challenges that may arise during the study. They can

troubleshoot problems, propose solutions, and work collaboratively with the study team to overcome obstacles.

7. **Regulatory compliance:** CRAs have a deep understanding of regulatory requirements and ensure that the study is conducted in accordance with applicable regulations and guidelines. This includes obtaining necessary approvals, maintaining accurate records, and reporting adverse events.

8. **Data integrity:** CRAs are responsible for monitoring and verifying the accuracy and completeness of study data. They conduct regular site visits, source document verification, and data validation to ensure data integrity.

9. **Continual learning:** CRAs stay updated on the latest developments in clinical research and regulatory requirements. They regularly

participate in training programs and professional development activities to enhance their knowledge and skills.

10. **Advocacy for participants:** CRAs advocate for the rights and well-being of study participants. They ensure that participants are fully informed about the study, their rights, and any potential risks or benefits. CRAs are dedicated to protecting the interests of participants throughout the research process.